bruegel

bruegel

Text by
JACQUES DOPAGNE

LEON AMIEL · PUBLISHER
NEW YORK

Published by
LEON AMIEL • PUBLISHER
NEW YORK
ISBN 0-8148-0641-4
Printed in the United States of America

"How can the human mind contain so much devilry and so many marvelous things?" wrote Baudelaire as he pondered Bruegel's work, Bruegel the Strange One as he preferred to call him and not the Elder, Pieter or the "Old Man" as we refer to him today distinguishing him from his two sons "Hell Bruegel" and "Velvet Bruegel". "What artist," insists Baudelaire, "could compose such monstrously paradoxical works, as if driven by some unknown force?" Referring to the famous *witches' epidemic* which raged during the sixteenth century, Baudelaire did not hesitate to express his intimate feelings for Bruegel as he did for

Paganini, the joker, fooling himself, so to speak, would have conversed with the Devil himself. No statement is more fitting to describe Bruegel's unusual and strange genius.

Indeed, although this genius is well known to us, that is, we can at least evaluate his work, we know very little about the person himself. Bruegel's life remains clouded in mystery. Little light has been shed on the circumstances under which he became aware of his talents, developed them, and how in a short period of 16 years reached his artistic peak. Nor do we know when or where the artist was born, any more than we are sure of the origin of his name, and that "Bruegel" is in fact a patronymic. Bruegel, spelled this way by the painter himself after 1559, may not represent a place bearing that name, for there are several in Holland.

At best we are reduced to certain hypotheses. One fact has been ascertained. In 1569, at little more than forty years of age, Bruegel's sparkling career came to an end.

As a youth he was the student of Pieter Coecke van Aelst, a famous painter from Antwerp. Indeed there is a similarity between the styles of the two artists. Nevertheless, whether Bruegel was actually an apprentice in Pieter Coecke's studio remains unproven, even though some writers take pleasure in assuring us that it was during this apprenticeship that Bruegel fell in love with his future wife—then still a child, none other than Pieter Coecke's daughter. It is equally certain that Bruegel worked in the studio of the painter Malines in 1550 practicing with water colors on canvas, a technique in which he later excelled (*The Misanthrope, The Parable of the Blind*). These various pieces of information relating to the years of Bruegel's apprenticeship attest in any case to the fact that in 1551 Bruegel still painted only in the employ of other painters. After 1551 Bruegel was no longer employed as a subordinate but became a Master in the Antwerp Painters Guild. However, the artist did not stay in Antwerp, and decided not to remain in any definite place. In the manner of other Dutch painters who wanted to seriously enhance their careers, he undertook his first trip to Italy (1551-1552).

There is little information about this trip except that after stopping in Lyon, Bruegel continued on to Rome, Naples, Reggio de Calabria, Messina and undoubtedly Palermo. Returning to Rome, he formed a friendship with the miniaturist Giulio Clovio, who, much older than Bruegel, became a protector and mentor for the artist. On the way back to Holland, Bruegel was especially impressed by the awe-inspiring spectacle of several Alpine landscapes. This fascination is exhibited in numerous works during his brief career, *(The Conversion of St. Paul, The Suicide of Saul)*. Many copies of these works were made by professional engravers which enhanced the artist's reputation and profited the merchants.

In 1563 Bruegel married Marie Coecke, the daughter of his former presumed master. At his future mother-in-law's insistance, Bruegel agreed to marry in Brussels rather than Antwerp. She felt that it was the only way that Bruegel would forget a mistress in Antwerp. Whatever the true reasons were Bruegel left Antwerp reluctantly since he had many friends in that city. In particular, Abraham Oertel (1527-1598), the famous historian and geographer. The depth of this man's admiration for Bruegel is readily evident from the epitaph he composed after the premature death of the painter. Oertel realized without question Bruegel's talent, and surmised his works would be shining examples in future centuries. His friendship, however, was not limited to his deep admiration for the artist. It was probably he who introduced Bruegel into the Club of Catholics, disciples of Erasmus, artists who by word and deed opposed all kinds of intolerance committed either by the Church or the State. Numerous designs, engravings and paintings by Bruegel mark this influence.

Although Bruegel left his friends in Antwerp with great reluctance, naturally giving up his daily encounters with them, he succeeded in acquiring many new friends in Brussels. Among others were the Cardinal of Granvelle, and the Archbishop of Malines, a famous collector who owned several important works by the painter. What was Bruegel's life in Brussels really like? To tell the truth, we don't know much about it; nor do we know whether marriage contributed to his being a happy man.

Considering all of the data about Bruegel and the fact that the documentary sources are so poor and often contradictory, there is practically no other solution than to consult his paintings. In the final analysis they alone shed some light. That is why in order to give the reader a real intimacy with the man Bruegel, we have decided to quickly analyze each one, of his works reproduced in this book.

1. *The Parable of the Sower*

This is the first signed and dated work by

Bruegel. Painted in the great landscape tradition, this painting, highly regarded at that time, has the foreground in brown, green and blue in the backgrounds, and shows Christ in the boat with a crowd of about thirty at the right on the banks. The parable itself, however, is told in the foreground. The sower is a man in his prime facing us. Behind him, near the first house are two bags of seed. It is for us to understand that one portion of this seed will not grow, but will be devoured by the birds. Another portion will fall on sterile ground and will hardly grow at all. Only the third portion will be planted in rich soil and grow to maturity. This painting was well known during Bruegel's lifetime as is attested to by the numerous engraved reproductions.

2-3. *The Fall of Icarus*

According to experts this painting describes the only mythological subject treated by Bruegel. It is also one of the rare examples in which the subject matter is not merely a pretext for showing off the landscape. Much has been written about Bruegel's interpretation of Ovid's fable. Icarus, a hero who symbolized the follies of the Middle Ages, has just fallen into the sea. His legs are still encompassed in a halo of foam, but nothing, either in the natural world or in the human one is paying the least attention to the drama unfolding about him. Sailors on their ships, a fisherman, shepherd, laborer—each one continues, unperturbed with his occupation. The question arises as to whether Bruegel intended two different interpretations for the painting, maybe complementing perhaps even contradicting one another. One possibility alludes to the German proverb which states that "no plough stops because of the death of a man." The second would simply translate the message of Ovid himself, that is, that one should know that moderation and the golden rule are the essential ingredients for happiness.

4. *Harbor of Naples*

What does this painting represent exactly? Certainly in the background it depicts the harbor of Naples as it must have been in the 16th century, pretty much as conceived by experts. But is that all? Is the naval battle significant? No, absolutely not. A skirmish perhaps, or something else? What we are sure of, on the other hand, is that whoever painted this work was skilled, and as in the preceding painting, the artist knew a great deal about ships, loved them and enjoyed painting even their smallest details with tremendous precision.

5-10. *Netherlandish Proverbs*

This painting brings us to the cycle of Bruegel's major works. Major, however, not by virtue of the quality in its execution. Other works by Bruegel are much better in composition and in general technique. What confers such force and authority on this painting, however, is the remarkable profusion of some 120 illustrated proverbs or popular maxims. Of course this moralizing style was in vogue in the 16th century, especially in Dutch speaking countries. Many artists conformed to this style but no one could, like Bruegel, exploit the existing "proverbial" literature with as much verve and critical judgment.

A crowd of people, comprised of artisans from the villages and workers from the field carrying their tools or animals, are also scrupulous interpreters of this gigantic Rabelaisian fable. On a superficial level we see each person, or sometimes a couple, perform his task, isolated from the others. The decor itself is arbitrary and there is no *plastic* bond to assure the unity of the whole. The painting does not depend on those features. Each individual fulfills his role so well that this lends a more subtle kind of unity resulting from the spirited fashion in which the artist leads the spectator to consider this accumulation of proverbs as a remedy for human folly. In the center of the painting is a couple which the artist has focused upon with particular care in order to represent in them a synthesis of all of the various human derangements: a beautiful young woman, portrait of elegance and draped in a sumptuous red dress (note that Bruegel never paints a woman nude) is different from the other more common people. He wraps her husband in a blue cape (blue symbolizes duplicity—or disloyalty while red may mean shamelessness) so that this spoiled, bandy-legged man would not realize he was being cuckolded. A globe of the earth, also blue, is placed upside down on a gallows at the left. The rogue wearing a harlequin hat above the window frame is without equivocation making light of what he had done. Christ, also dressed in blue, is a victim of treachery by a monk who has placed him on a red throne and is trying a false blond beard on him (a sign of mockery). As for those two above the river that we see relieving themselves in the same hole, they might illustrate the French dictum "necessity makes the laws." And so on, until all the protagonists are accounted for.

11-15. *The Fight Between Carnival and Lent*

Here is a painting in which the magic of color transcends the numerous stories, and works forcefully upon the viewer to engage his interest in the swarms of people of all types and social classes. They are painted realistically and not in the heavy marionette style which impeded the figures in the *Netherlandish Proverbs*. It is relatively easy to decipher the theme which was inspired by a medieval fable and had already influenced Hieronymous Bosch. In one of the two camps, the fat Carnival character (the Prostestant Church according to some exegetes) sits astride a barrel as fat as himself, with pans instead of stirrups, a paté for a headdress, and a spear running through a suckling pig. Following him are some grotesque characters all in disguise; representing every imaginable vice and all forms of gluttony. Everyone is engaged in the pleasures of eating, drinking and fornication while the poor beggars and the handicapped are left to their misery. See also Painting 63 *The Beggars*. In the other camp is the thin Lent (the Catholic Church) represented by an old emaciated woman sitting in a wagon driven by a monk and a nun on the way to the attack. She is armed with a shovel, in which two herrings are virtuously laid out, to defend herself against the blows of Carnival. The crowd behind, unlike those with Carnival, are eating a small ration of food and seem hardly aggressive. Also in this part of the painting each person is involved in some worthwhile action. What seems clear in any case is that Bruegel does not take sides in this battle. Or perhaps he does, but in a unique way: the couple in the center who are going in the opposite direction from the rest of the people are completely disassociated from everything happening about them, as if to tell us, all things being equal "those people are really stupid."

16-18. *Children's Games*

In this painting depicting the games of some 200 children, Bruegel is really attacking grown-ups. Only their size and dress make them children. When five of them start pulling the hair of their victim or killing flies, they behave as adults. Furthermore, there is not a single face among them expressing joy or the fun of playing a game. Their movements are restrained, like some gnomes or puppets manipulated by some invisible force, closer to madness than to childhood. At the top of the painting on the left is a landscape free of human pollution where anyone can escape into the fresh air. This foreshadows an idea that became very important to Bruegel in some of his later works, namely, that nature alone can redeem the world from the follies of mankind.

19. *Fight of Peasants*

Several works on this subject were made. In this one, the date and signature are not clear (perhaps by one of Bruegel's sons), although the style belongs to the master himself. And this battle among the peasants which is followed by that miserable card game recalls a number of analogies with the faces and movements in the preceding painting, *Children's Games*. The same is true for the next three paintings. Who are the adults and who are the children?

20, 23. *The Peasant Dance*

On one level of this excellent painting, people are dancing, playing, eating, drinking and kissing. The main couple are not dancing yet but are hurrying with an air of impetuousness to join the dance. Nevertheless, if you look closely, these people are not as happy as they seem. On the left are two children who look and behave like adults imitating their elders like many children in Bruegel's paintings. For the music there is only one piper. And beside him a young man is encouraging him without any real enthusiasm and offering him a big pitcher of beer. Around the table people are eating and drinking and the alcohol is certainly helping some of them come to blows. Behind them are a couple kissing joylessly. Likewise the other couples in the background; they too are dancing without any real joy. The unity of this painting underscores the masterful technique in the composition and use of color. This technique was certainly suited for the sensitive rendering of an oppressive atmosphere which so characterized Bruegel. The celebration in which all of these villagers are participating brings little joy to either their faces or their souls.

21. *The Wedding Dance*

The frenzied abandon in this dance provides us with a complete study of human nature. Here, people are giving in to unrestrained gluttony and sexual liberties, notably evidenced by the three men dancing in the foreground. (Over a period of many years this part has been expurgated, having been repainted in darker tones to flatten the trousers area so that this painting has little of its primitive veracity.) Look at the couple kissing. They remind us of the couple in

The Peasant Dance but not quite as joyless. As for the solitary spectator standing beside the two musicians, carrying an inkstand in his belt (mark of an educated man), he may well represent Bruegel's thoughts about the unleashing of instincts among these commoners. Perhaps he regards these villagers with more curiosity and scepticism than real sympathy or merely with a sense of complacency.

22, 24. *The Wedding Banquet*

No painting of Bruegel's has aroused more commentary than this one. Regarding the title or the subject, is it about a wedding meal? Because just as in the preceding painting (21), one of the two newlyweds is certainly identifiable, the married woman, an ugly-ruddy-looking girl, plump and smiling and sitting alone under a wall hanging with her hands folded in an awkward manner. Many experts have in various ways justified the absence of the young man who is not in this scene near his new wife. Others assert, and this seems like a more plausible explanation, that the young man, according to the Dutch customs in certain villages, is none other than the sympathetic fellow, who with much ease and unsophistication is gathering the plates onto the trays (the heavy door, unhinged for the occasion is supported by two strong merry lads) and passing the food toward his wife and guests.

Whatever interpretation, this scene elicits a satirical perspective. The satire is reinforced by the attitude of the little girl in the foreground who is busily licking the left-overs, unaware of what is going on around her. Also the servant behind her who never seems to finish filling up the beer mugs. In any case not a single guest is concerned with the spiritual aspects of the occasion. That's what the monk, the bearded character with folded hands at the far right, seems to say as he sits there feigning attention. Note, too, the sign of vanity for the entire scene, the peacock's feather the little girl's hair and also in the young man admiring the musician (in no. 20). The peacock's feather in Bruegel's time symbolized vanity.

25-26. *The Numbering at Bethlehem*

What strikes us in this painting is the description of the daily events in a Flemish village during winter, when the red sun slowly rises in a cloudy, cold sky above the dark branches of a huge desolate tree. Here again Bruegel asserts one of his important ideas. Everything in the composition—human beings, animals, objects and even the landscape—which is rare for Bruegel, all are plunged into the stream of life in an anonymous way. The evangelical characters themselves hardly escape this rule. Joseph and Mary are two characters like the others, and passively submit to the population census and taxation. Not completely, however, if we look at them closely. They are distinguished by their position in the crowd, Mary's blue coat, Joseph's attitude, and by the close association between the ox and the donkey. In the middle at the right, the little dilapidated hut topped by a cross, seems to indicate that it is ready to fulfill its biblical role for the birth of the Savior, meaning that in some way it is the instrument of Destiny through which these people, while anonymous, take their place in history.

27-28. *The Dark Day*

This painting perhaps belongs to the famous "Seasons" Series in which some experts delight in placing several other paintings by Bruegel, of which we will speak later on. *The Dark Day* is a mysterious work because of its composition as well as the interpretation of its different sections. At first glance, however, and for the short time the eye concentrates on the foreground at the right, it all seems easy to decipher: the child who carries the lantern, undoubtedly because at this time of year the days are still very short, seems to bear the traditional crown of the Three Wise Men, while the peasant on the right eats the equally traditional biscuit. The others, on the left are going about the activities which mark the season, one of them making a bundle of firewood, and the other pruning a willow tree. Over all of this looms the disquieting threat of a storm. The menacing black sky projects faint flashes of catastrophe on the rough sea and frozen mountainsides. A veiled silent threat seems to hang heavily, particularly over the poor houses nestled on the left at the end of the valley. The two great discoveries in this painting are in the white, milky echo that constitutes the facade of the cottage in the snowy mountains of the background, and in the black silhouette made by the trees standing alone under the chiaroscuro stormy effects of the horizon.

29. *Storm at Sea*

This painting reflects a similar climate, although the style is more typical of Bruegel's later works, which are more reserved and syncopated as well. Certain exegetes have suggested that this painting was meant to illustrate the proverb of the whale who abandons the ship in order to fall on the cask floating before her (the equivalent of our modern dictum "to drop the substance for the shadow"). For other specialists, another interpretation would be to compare the fate of man in general to that of the crew of the threatened ship, who if they agreed to sacrifice their material goods, might escape danger and gain salvation as symbolized by the church located in the clearing on the horizon. In any event the savage beauty of this painting is not in its esoterism. The dramatic tone, as in Moby Dick, which characterizes this work is enough.

30-34. *The Fall of the Rebel Angels*

This painting, which for a long time was thought to have been done by either Hieronymus Bosch or Hell Bruegel until a carefully executed screening revealed its real author, borrows evidently its general design from the idealism of Bosch, branding once again the folly of men (or their demons) in conflict with the spirit of good. In the center, Saint Michael, young and slender under his coat of armor, is assisted by two angels who, unimpeded, dominate the upper section of the painting, while on the bottom swarms the monstrous band of fallen angels.

35-37. *Dulle Griet*

Many remarks have been made to the effect that of all of Bruegel's works, this one bears the greatest similarity to those of Bosch. Certainly, like Bosch, there are in this extraordinary composition monsters, demons, a frightful collection of ruins, incendiaries, collapsing towers, disturbing grottos. Everything representing the horrors of those times finds an account here. At this point the resemblance to Bosch ends. One should bear in mind that precisely at this time the Netherlands submitted to the miserable occupation of the Spanish and that the opposition to the invader became more and more virulent. Whatever the intent, the work is obviously subject to several interpretations. Among all of these fantastic creatures, born of fear and anguish, is the giant Dulle Griet (Crazy or Wild Margot), helmeted and clad in iron armor, with a broad, decisive step, strides along, sword in hand, staring distractedly. Her wide, open mouth shouts a cry of oppression. In a large cloth tied by a knot she nimbly carries the strange fruits of unreasoned pillaging, completely indifferent to the ruin she brings around her. This apocalyptic figure undoubtedly symbolizes a violent, oppressive spirit. In fact certain commentators have remarked that this work foreshadowed Picasso's *Guernica*. This is understandable and we agree with them.

38-44. *The Triumph of Death*

For Bruegel, death is the result of sinning rather than the natural outcome of human fragility. In any case this painting is certainly one of the most horrible ever conceived by the imagination depicting man's fear of death. Such an obsessive prolificity with this theme is "quasi-diabolical", to paraphrase Baudelaire. Indeed, since Bruegel's time we have become experts in matters of terror. And today reality joins fiction. Who can envy Bruegel, when we think of the great slaughter at Verdun and the atrocious genocide by the Nazis in their extermination camps? But to come back to this painting, it is so rich in details and symbolic meaning that it would require pages and pages to adequately describe.

45. *Two Monkeys*

This painting, in very reduced dimensions, symbolizes without doubt the submission of the Flemish kingdom to the Spanish occupation—

which, however, does not prevent the simultaneous representation of man enslaved by sin. Besides the two interpretations are not contradictory. Looking at these two monkeys sadly sitting on the ledge of a large window whose arch is so low that it would surely remind one of a prison. The two animals are chained to a single central ring, in a position of great overwhelming sadness. Behind them, in a grayish-red light, the port and town of Antwerp are recognizable. In the foreground at the right two empty nut shells most certainly illustrate the medieval dictum, "many men sell their liberty for a hazel nut." The details are like those in the foreground at the right in *The Peasant Dance* (20). The monkeys, like men, are often trapped by their desire for trivial things. Similarly, the two monkeys who are prisoners behind the bars in the facade of the foreground at the right of *Dulle Griet* (37).

46-47. *The Conversion of St. Paul*

No other work of Bruegel's contains so many spatial suggestions: in the distance, in the deep grooves in the rocks, one sees the beginning of an immense plain, and coming from there, the Duke of Alba's army crossing the Alps to crush the revolt brewing in Holland. Officially, of course, the subject of the painting concerns something else. However, upon reflection, this subject seems to be simply a pretext: the sudden conversion of this bearded, unpolished captain, who later became Saint Paul, represents the long and painful path to truth—marked here by the accumulation of material difficulties. Bruegel has piled up in this description, all of the aspects of the long ascension, interminable it would appear, up the escarpments and all along the most sinister of Alpine gorges. The point of departure, on the left, comes from afar in the fog covering the plain. The arrival seems nowhere to be visible, the enormous army is lost among the dark gorges in the innermost recesses of the mountain.

48. *The Suicide of Saul*

The Philistine army is about to conquer and demolish the Israelites. Saul, wearing armor and crown on his head, is wounded and isolated on a small platform (on the left), threatened with imminent capture. He throws himself on his sword, and precipitates the same action by his servant. The entire foreground at the right is full of victorious Philistines, an incredible swarm of locusts and of Israelites fleeing. Note the dazzling *impressionist* manner with which this part of the painting is treated. In the center, on the cliff, a horrible massacre has just taken place, probably of Saul's sons. As for the decor in which the battle unfolds, Bruegel was inspired by the grandiose impressions that he retained of the Alps on his trip to Italy.

49-51. *The Procession to Calvary*

This is without doubt Bruegel's best painting. It is also among those in which the artist intended to illustrate what was considered man's most serious offense to God, indifference. Therefore, in the foreground, aside from the group of holy women, the entire atmosphere projects a sort of kermis, with, however, the vultures hovering in the dark sky as they search for their prey on the gallows. The crowd accompanying Jesus to His torture is less than five hundred. The long, disorderly train is escorted along by armed Spanish soldiers in red dress who are trying to guide in a single direction. Some idle gapers join the crowd near Simon the Cyrenean (in the middle on the left), who is held by his wife as he tries to resist the commands of the sbirros. As for Jesus, who has just collapsed under the burden of the cross, (in the center of the painting), He is completely lost, alone, and generally indifferent, although in the distance under the gibbets and the gallows appears the arid and sterile mount of death.

52. *The Tower of Babel* (1)

The theme in the Tower of Babel interested Bruegel very much. In this painting the artist again intends to demonstrate men's folly. With whatever zeal, like real ants they undertake a task, the hope for success is denied them. Bruegel gives an excellent illustration here. At the same level where the construction is taking place, there is one section which seems finished to the last detail, but is in fact in contradiction technically with another section where nothing has begun as yet. This automatically suggests the idea of the inexorability of time. An inexorability against which no order can prevail, including those of the proud king Nimrod who struggles in vain to impose his orders on his workers.

53. *The Tower of Babel* (2)

In this painting which is twice as small as the preceding one, the tower, with its close-up view, is a monumental achievement, being both more stark and more somber. King Nimrod is absent. The sin of pride is emphasized in a clearer fashion by the lonely presence of the edifice whose upper part, also incomplete, is a menacing dark red, while the heavy-hanging clouds, darker than in the first painting, further increases the impression of general malaise.

54-55. *Haymaking*

No one has yet confirmed for certain that this painting as well as *The Harvesters, The Return of the Herd, The Dark Day* and *Hunters in the Snow* are part of the series dedicated to the twelve months of the year. (This would imply that seven other paintings have disappeared.) However, this is unimportant. What is essential for us, on the other hand, is the intrinsic beauty of each work. In this one, whose atmosphere is especially transparent and so beautifully evokes the joy usually associated with this type of subject, what do we see? In the background of a very calm landscape dominated by greens, the foreground accentuates an opposite rhythm. Here are the fruit carriers passing in front of a post which is crowned with a grove dedicated to the Virgin, and on the same diagonal are three young girls carrying rakes as they move towards the left where a peasant is sharpening his scythe. The whole painting presents a lively picture of nature to which is added the feelings of all of the people, whether they are nearby or in the distance—as they show a sincere *joie de vivre* and real happiness.

56. *The Harvesters*

This painting is dominated by golds and ochres, not greens. Nevertheless a similar *joie de vivre* exists. More awkward perhaps especially in the section around the sleeping peasant at the foot of the tree who looks like the brother of the one happily eating in *The Land of Cockaigne* (57). Once again, and as in each painting which comprises this admirable series, the man appears without any anecdote to illustrate, and occupies a place in the world which he has succeeded in acquiring, a place which suits him, and to which he is still entitled today.

57. *The Land of Cockaigne*

This translated a Dutch text of that period describing in detail the famous Cockaigne region. The book says everything that Bruegel wanted to illustrate: "This land until today has only been visited by rascals who discovered it in the first place. All who want to go there must be completely fearless and ready to meet great challenges, because in the front if a very high and long mountain of Saracen dough, across which they must *eat* before arriving in that well-known region. Cockaigne is famous for its unsavory characters and those who have forsaken all virtue and decency. For there is no greater shame in this land than to behave virtuously, reasonably, honorably and with good manners. In fact, whoever acts in a virtuous way is hated by everybody else and eventually is banished from the country."

58-59. *The Return of the Herd*

From a first glance we see two parallel diagonals, the reddish flock, and the green stream which leads the eye from the lower right angle along a very marked ascending line towards the top left: The feverish stamping of the flock in the middle on the left as they fade into the depths of the autumnal landscape surrounded here and there by bare trees, the painting majestically evokes the time when the flock returns to the stalls.

60. *Hunters in the Snow*

This painting is without any doubt the culminating one of the series, as if it were somehow the height of accomplishment. The style is held in such great esteem that it goes far beyond the subject matter. Bruegel supports the idea here, more than in any other work, of the total submission of man to the pressures of the natural world. In this severe and pure landscape the artist confronts a world which he feels, sees, measures and interprets as if it were a living organism. Brown, gray and green are the only colors which connote cold, peace and silence. The immeasurable silence which suffocates children's voices on the frozen ponds, which burdens tired hunters, which dotes on hungry dogs and which accompanies the flight of crows in the cold air. "Never," wrote one critic, "has one rendered with such intensity the poetry of a northern landscape with its dismal melancholy; and this is captured with marvelous clarity, without foggy sentimentality, without complications: this feat is rare in painting the North."

61. *The Magpie on the Gallows*

Some experts interpret this painting as another challenge hurled at the Spanish oppressor. It could also have been titled, "Dancing under the Gallows," or more exactly, as the Flemish proverb says, "To relieve oneself under the Gallows," as is demonstrated by the peasant who is about to relieve himself in the lower left corner. For other critics it is the magpie, symbol of slander and calumny, which gives meaning to this composition. These two interpretations are not at all incompatible, if we admit that that denouncement easily follows from slander. From there to the gallows and as suggested slightly to the right, to the tomb. But Bruegel's message to us leaves a ray of hope. No amount of torture, gallows or persecution will make these people lose their joy of living. The proof being that these peasants are dancing. Also the colors of their costumes are gay. And above all, to prolong the idea of this zest for life, is a fantastic landscape which stretches beyond the undulations in the foreground to infinity.

62. *The Birdnesters*

For most of the critics this painting illustrates above all else the proverb, "one who *sees* the nest knows about it, but he who *takes* it, has it in his possession." On the contrary, for others who regard the young peasant in the foreground as about to fall into the stream, like in the Gospel according to Saint Matthew, this painting refers to the passage, "why beholdest thou the mote that is in thy brother's eye, but considerest not the beam that is in thine own eye?" It is agreed

that this statement is completely within the
moralizing and pessimistic sense that is usual
with Bruegel. But what does that matter to us?
What matters is the delightful character of this
painting which makes one think of Corot and
Courbet, as it has both *impressionist* and *ex-
pressionist* qualities.

63. *The Beggars*

First of all, this group of helpless people and
the manner in which they are depicted is not
unique with Bruegel. For example, look at the
unfortunates similarly treated in the middle portion slightly to the right in *The Fight between
Carnival and Lent* (13). But be careful in inter-
preting this small work (the smallest probably
that Bruegel ever painted). The artist surely did
not paint this amazing group to serve the in-
terests of these unfortunates. Their faces (even
as we might guess, the faces of those who turn
their backs to us) express the contrary. What we
know now with some certainty is that the foxes'
tails that each of these "specimens of mankind"
is wearing was the mark in the middle ages of a
leper. And perhaps should we see in this master-
piece, aside from its truthful and objective
manner of presenting human degeneracy, is a
barely-disguised reference as is frequent with

Bruegel, to another form of decadence, which is the moral and within each man.

64-67. *The Parable of the Blind*

For this painting, comparable in dramatic intensity to the preceding one, Bruegel borrows once again from the text of Saint Matthew to emphasize the depths of his pessimism. It seems to say to us "what is the use of these men helping one another since they are all blind, and the one leading them, also blind, is inevitably condemned to fall first, and then to drag his companions after him into the muddy waters of the brook." The composition of this painting has been carefully planned and is completely based on the effects of the parallel diagonals which descend towards the right. The serene beauty of the landscape, the foggy aspects, and as indifferent as the Church in the distance, the empty world of these miserable creatures, their wild-looking appearance, the tension that is felt in the minutes before their fall, the muted range of colors—all of these things contribute to make this painting one of the most heart-rending works that western art has produced.

68-70. *The Misanthrope*

This painting, in the form of a medallion as

often in the case of Hieronymus Bosch, is one of the rare ones, along with the *Parable of the Blind* that Bruegel painted on canvas, not in oils as we said above. It is also among the rare, if not the only one, in which Bruegel himself has done the literary explanation in calligraphy. Unfortunately, the clarity of this text is relative, "Because the world is treacherous, I am going to wear a suit of mourning." Well, why then does this misanthrope who apparently has decided to renounce the world and sacrifice himself; the path before him is paved with thorns, why is he carrying his money? To tempt the thief imprisoned in a glass ball (symbol of the world)? To tell the truth, this painting can imply some other meaning. It might be a faintly disguised criticism directed against the avid nature of certain ecclesiastics. An interpretation which would explain the round format of the painting. The old man, as greedy as the pickpocket who robs him, would also be a prisoner of a glass world, that is, a world dedicated hopelessly to vice and perversity. The only ray of light in this particularly pessimistic painting is the faithful shepherd in the background, placed straight above the sphere of evil doings as he serenely watches his sheep in a typical Flemish countryside.

LIST OF PLATES

1 The Parable of the Sower 1557
Timken Art Gallery
San Diego, California

2-3 The Fall of Icarus 1558
Royal Museum of Fine Arts
Brussels

4 Harbor of Naples 1558
Doria Gallery
Rome

5-10 Netherlandish Proverbs 1559
Staatliche Museum
Berlin

11-15 The Fight between Carnival and Lent 1559
Kunsthistorisches Museum
Vienna

16-18 Children's Games 1559
Kunsthistorisches Museum
Vienna

19 Scuffle of the Peasants 1566
Fabre Museum
Montpellier

20, 23 The Peasant Dance 1568
Kunsthistorisches Museum
Vienna

21 The Wedding Dance 1566
Institute of Art
Detroit

22, 24 The Wedding Banquet 1568
Kunsthistorisches Museum
Vienna

25-26 The Numbering at Bethlehem 1566
Royal Museum of Fine Arts
Brussels

27-28 The Dark Day 1565
Kunsthistorisches Museum
Vienna

29 Storm at Sea 1568
Kunsthistorisches Museum
Vienna

30-34 The Fall of the Rebel Angels 1562
Royal Museum of Fine Arts
Brussels

35-37 Dulle Griet 1563
Mayer Van den Bergh Museum
Antwerp

38-44 The Triumph of Death 1563
Prado
Madrid

45 Two Monkeys 1562
Staatliche Museum
Berlin

46-47 The Conversion of St. Paul 1567
Kunsthistorisches Museum
Vienna

48 The Suicide of Saul 1562
Kunsthistorisches Museum
Vienna

49-51 The Procession to Calvary 1564
Kunsthistorisches Museum
Vienna

52 The Tower of Babel (1) 1563
Kunsthistorisches Museum
Vienna

53 The Tower of Babel (2) 1563
Boymans van Beuningen
Rotterdam

54-55 Haymaking 1565
Narodni Gallery
Prague

56 The Harvesters 1565
Metropolitan Museum
New York

57 The Land of Cockaigne 1567
   Alte Pinakothek
   Munich

58-59 The Return of the Herd 1565
   Kunsthistorisches Museum
   Vienna

60 Hunters in the Snow 1565
   Kunsthistorisches Museum
   Vienna

61 The Magpie on the Gallows 1568
   Landesmuseum
   Darmstadt

62 The Birdnesters 1568
   Kunsthistorisches Museum
   Vienna

63 The Beggars 1568
   Louvre
   Paris

64-67 The Parable of the Blind 1568
   Capodimonte National Gallery
   Naples

68-70 The Misanthrope 1568
   Capodimonte National Gallery
   Naples

PLATES

1
The Parable of the Sower
1557

2
The Fall of Icarus (detail)
1558

3
The Fall of Icarus
1558

4
Harbor of Naples
1558

5
Netherlandish Proverbs
1559

Netherlandish Proverbs (detail)
1559

7
Netherlandish Proverbs (detail)
1559

8

Netherlandish Proverbs (detail)
1559

9
Netherlandish Proverbs (detail)
1559

10
Netherlandish Proverbs (detail)
1559

11
The Fight between Carnival and Lent (detail)
1559

12
The Fight between Carnival and Lent (detail)
1559

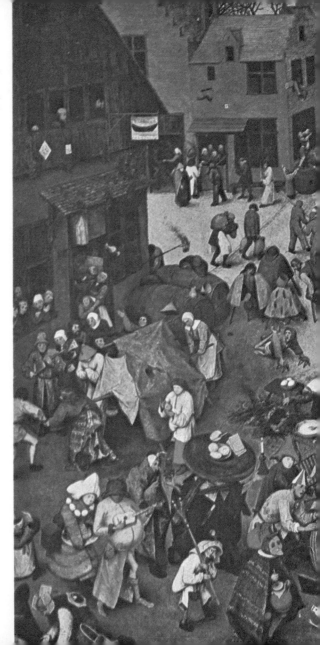

13
The Fight between
Carnival and Lent
1559

14
The Fight between Carnival and Lent (detail)
1559

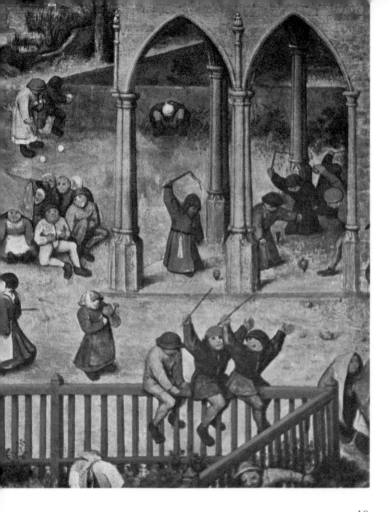

16
Children's Games (detail)
1559

17
Children's Games (detail)
1559

18
Children's Games
1559

19
Scuffle of the Peasants
1566

20
The Peasant Dance
1568

21
The Wedding Dance
1566

The Peasant Dance (detail)
1568

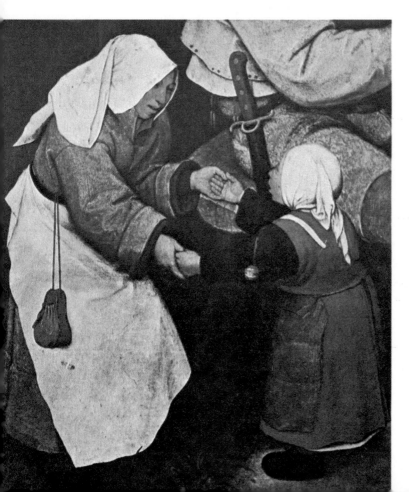

24
The Wedding Banquet (detail)
1568

25
The Numbering at Bethlehem (detail)
1566

26
The Numbering at Bethlehem
1566

27
The Dark Day
1565

28
The Dark Day (detail)
1565

29
Storm at Sea
1568

The Fall of the Rebel Angels
1562

31-32
The Fall of the Rebel Angels (detail)
1562

33
The Fall of the Rebel Angels
(detail) 1562

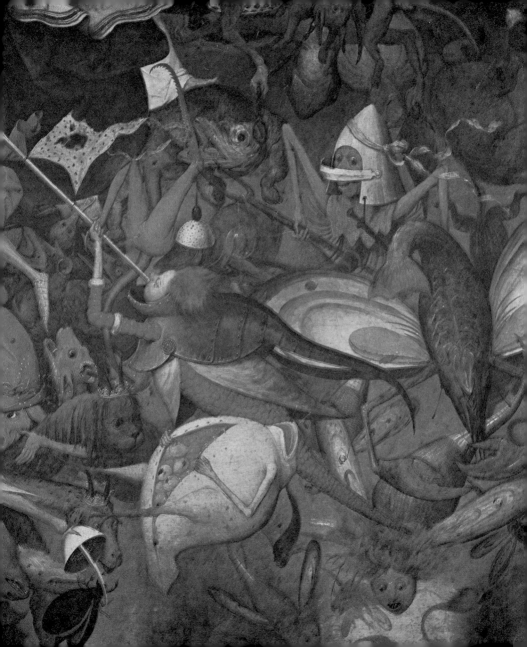

34
The Fall of the Rebel
Angels (detail) 1562

35-36
Dulle Griet (detail)
1563

37
Dulle Griet
1563

The Triumph of Death (detail)
1563

40
The Triumph of Death (detail)
1563

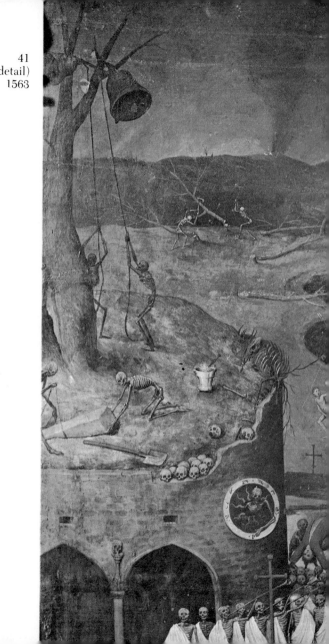

41
The Triumph of Death (detail)
1563

43
The Triumph of Death (detail)
1563

BRVEGEL · MDLXII

45
Two Monkeys
1562

46
The Conversion of St. Paul
1567

47
The Conversion of St. Paul (detail)
1567

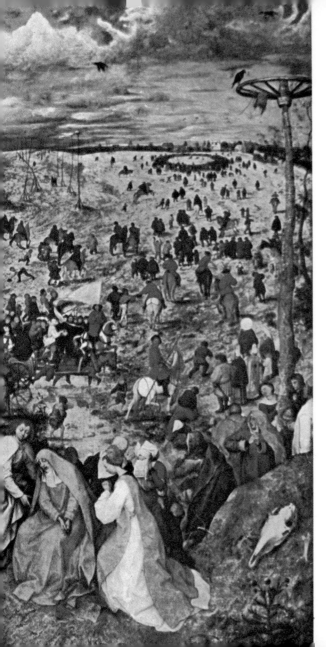

49
The Procession to Calvary
1564

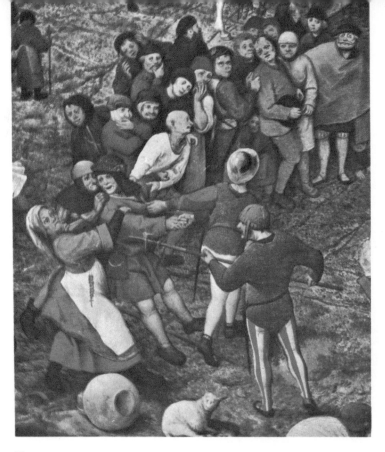

50
The Procession to Calvary (detail)
1564

51
The Procession to Calvary (detail)
1564

52

The Tower of Babel (1)
1563

53
The Tower of Babel (2)
1563

54
Haymaking (detail)
1565

55
Haymaking
1565

57
The Land of Cockaigne
1567

59
The Return of the Herd (detail)
1565

60
Hunters in the Snow
1565

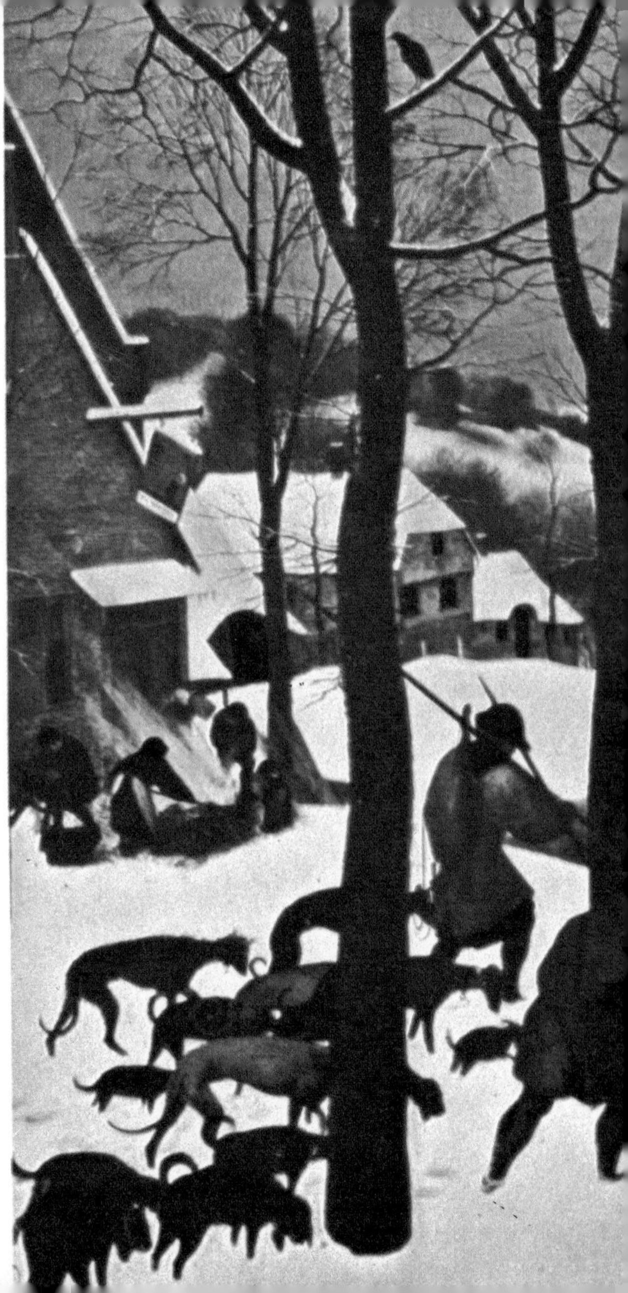

61
The Magpie on the Gallows
1568

62
The Birdnesters
1568

63
The Beggars
1568

64
The Parable of the Blind
1568

65
The Parable of the Blind (detail)
1568

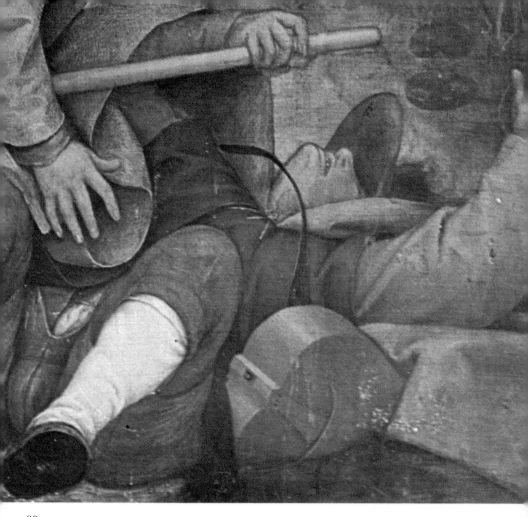

66
The Parable of the Blind (detail)
1568

67
The Parable of the Blind (detail)
1568

68
The Misanthrope (detail)
1568

69
The Misanthrope (detail)
1568